P9-CRJ-854

INTRO TO
DRESSAGE

BY WHITNEY SANDERSON

SADDLE UP!

SportsZone

An Imprint of Abdo Publishing
abdopublishing.com

abdopublishing.com

Published by Abdo Publishing, a division of ABDO, PO Box 398166, Minneapolis, Minnesota 55439. Copyright © 2018 by Abdo Consulting Group, Inc. International copyrights reserved in all countries. No part of this book may be reproduced in any form without written permission from the publisher. SportsZone™ is a trademark and logo of Abdo Publishing.

Printed in the United States of America, North Mankato, Minnesota
092017
012018

Cover Photo: Friso Gentsch/picture-alliance/dpa/AP Images
Interior Photos: Friso Gentsch/picture-alliance/dpa/AP Images, 1; Ron Burton/Keystone/ Hulton Archives/Getty Images, 5; Getty Images Sport/Getty Images, 6; Keystone Pictures USA/Alamy, 7; Arterra/Universal Images Group/Getty Images, 9; Album/Prisma/ Newscom, 11; Photo12/Universal Images Group/Getty Images, 12–13; AP Images, 15; Attila Volgyi Xinhua News Agency/Newscom, 16; Jochen Luebke/AFP/DDP/Getty Images, 18–19; Olivia Harris/Reuters/Newscom, 20; Adam Ihse/Scanpix/AP Images, 22; John Rich/ iStockphoto, 25; iStockphoto, 27, 37, 38; Greg Philpott/Alamy, 29; Shutterstock Images, 30–31; Lee Beel/Alamy, 34–35; Bai Xuefei Xinhua News Agency/Newscom, 40–41; Charles Bertram/Lexington Herald-Leader/AP Images, 43; Jon Stroud/Rex Features/AP Images, 44

Editor: Marie Pearson
Series Designer: Laura Polzin
Content Consultant: Paige Clark, B.S. Equine Science, University of Minnesota Crookston

Publisher's Cataloging-in-Publication Data
Names: Sanderson, Whitney, author.
Title: Intro to dressage / by Whitney Sanderson.
Description: Minneapolis, Minnesota : Abdo Publishing, 2018. | Series: Saddle up! |
    Includes online resources and index.
Identifiers: LCCN 2017946871 | ISBN 9781532113390 (lib.bdg.) | ISBN 9781532152276
    (ebook)
Subjects: LCSH: Dressage--Juvenile literature. | Horsemanship--Juvenile literature. |
    Horse sports--Juvenile literature.
Classification: DDC 798.23--dc23
LC record available at https://lccn.loc.gov/2017946871

TABLE OF
CONTENTS

1

ART AND WAR: THE HISTORY OF DRESSAGE

A crowd of people watched a woman on a glossy bay horse canter across a sand arena. With every stride, the horse changed the leg it was leading with so that it appeared to be skipping. The lead leg is the foreleg that strikes the ground last. The people in the audience looked closely, trying to see the woman signal the horse. But she sat tall and still in the saddle.

Lis Hartel grew up riding horses.

Jubilee was 11 years old at the Helsinki Games.

The rider was Lis Hartel of Denmark. The horse was a mare named Jubilee. They were in Helsinki, Finland, for the 1952 Olympic Games. It was the first year that women were allowed to compete with men in any equestrian sport. It was also the first year the games were open to riders who were not in their country's military.

Jubilee weighed approximately 1,000 pounds (450 kg), but she looked feather-light as she crossed the arena. She lengthened her stride so that she seemed to be floating on air. Then she shortened her steps so that she moved up and down like a carousel horse. She trotted sideways across the arena. Her front and hind legs crossed in front of each other. Still, no one could see the commands that Hartel gave to Jubilee.

Hartel and Jubilee, *left*, went on to win a second Olympic silver in 1956. Henri Saint Cyr, *center*, won gold again, and Liselott Linsenhoff took bronze.

The pair trotted down the centerline of the arena and halted. Hartel saluted to the judges. The audience applauded. It was a beautiful round.

The ride earned them the silver medal. At the awards ceremony, the winner, Henri Saint Cyr of Sweden, lifted Hartel from Jubilee's back and helped her stand on the podium. Hartel could not walk on her own. At the age of 23, she was paralyzed by polio.

THERAPEUTIC RIDING

Hartel promoted using horses to provide therapy for people with disabilities. Today, people around the world receive therapy from horses.

People wondered how Hartel could get Jubilee to listen so well when her own movement was so limited. Over the years, Hartel and Jubilee built a relationship that let the mare sense the smallest cues from her rider. Hartel could use slight shifts of her seat and thighs instead of her lower leg and heel. Jubilee's sensitive mouth allowed Hartel to give soft rein signals without needing a strong grip. The pair showed the value of softness and harmony when working with horses.

ON THE BATTLEFIELD

Dressage began as a way to prepare horses for war. In ancient Greece and Rome, horses had to obey their riders even during the chaos of battle. They needed to listen

Ancient soldiers sometimes held a sword or spear in one hand and a shield in the other.

to their rider's legs and seat because one or both of a soldier's hands might be filled with weapons.

In 350 BCE, the Greek soldier Xenophon wrote *The Art of Horsemanship*. It is the earliest known book about horse training. Xenophon believed that gentle methods were the best. He said that a horse should move as proudly and freely under saddle as if it were at liberty.

After Xenophon, not much was written on the subject for centuries. In medieval Europe, the use of heavy armor made horses slower and less responsive. Fine horsemanship was not as important as it had once been.

But in the 1500s, the noble classes of Italy, Spain, and France grew interested in classical riding again. They may have been influenced by the swift, agile Arab warhorses that European Christians encountered while battling Muslims between 1095 and 1291.

Antoine de Pluvinel was the horse master for King Louis VIII. In the late 1500s and early 1600s, Pluvinel

The Arab warhorses were not weighed down with heavy armor, allowing them to be quick and responsive.

M. de Potrin.

Figure 6.   1 partie.

invented a new training method. He tied the horse between two pillars. Then he taught the horse to trot in place without moving forward. This training caused the horse's strides to become light and powerful. Also, its neck had a beautiful arch. This is because the horse is using all of its muscles during this exercise.

In the 1730s, François Robichon de la Guérinière of France first wrote about advanced movements such as *tempi* changes, in which the horse changes its leading foot with every canter stride, that are found in dressage tests today.

Horses built muscle when Pluvinel taught them to trot in place.

2

HORSES IN HARMONY: DRESSAGE TODAY

By the start of World War II (1939–1945), tanks had mostly replaced horses in war. People outside of the military began learning dressage. They organized horse shows across Europe. In the 1960s and 1970s, dressage spread to the United States. Riders imported dressage horses from Sweden, Denmark, and other countries. Hilda Gurney and her Thoroughbred Keen were an influential pair in the

Dressage grew in popularity during the mid-1900s.

United States during the 1970s. Keen proved that horses other than warmbloods could be successful in dressage. Today, people can still see how dressage was used in the military. The Spanish Riding School in Vienna, Austria, trains stallions to perform difficult moves for audiences.

The main organizations for dressage in North America are the United States Equestrian Federation (USEF) and the United States Dressage Federation (USDF). The USEF also oversees other equine sports, such as show jumping and eventing. The USDF specializes in dressage. The rules for international shows are set by the Fédération Équestre Internationale (FEI).

The USEF and USDF levels of competition begin at Training, followed by First, Second, Third, and Fourth levels. Each level has several official tests. USDF members can gather points to earn bronze, silver, and gold medals as they move up. The FEI levels are Prix St-Georges; Intermediate I, A, B, and II; and Grand Prix, which asks for more difficult movements than a Fourth Level test.

A Lipizzaner performs a levade at the Spanish Riding School.

Some dressage shows also have special classes. The quadrille is a test for at least four riders, and the pas de deux is a test for two riders. The freestyle is a dressage test set to music. Riders must include certain movements, but they have freedom to craft their own routine. Many riders use classical music, but others get creative with jazz or rock and roll.

THE MOVEMENTS

Dressage asks for three basic gaits: walk, trot, and canter. Training level dressage tests ask for "working" gaits. These should be brisk and even, but not rushed. The horse also performs figures such as circles and changes of direction. The rider might

Riders wearing historic costumes perform a quadrille at the FEI World Equestrian Games in 2006.

practice doing figure eights and three-loop serpentines to get the horse to bend. Bending helps the horse be relaxed and responsive to the rider. Most of the time, the horse's nose should be turned slightly to the inside of the ring. Its body should curve slightly into each corner or circle.

There are two quarter lines: one on each side of the centerline.

The rider's main aids, or ways of signaling to the horse, are the legs, seat, and hands. If the horse's attention begins to drift, the rider can use a half-halt. This aid combines a gentle squeeze on the reins with slight leg pressure to remind the horse to listen and balance.

After the training level, dressage tests ask for collected (shortened) and extended (lengthened) gaits. At First Level and up, tests ask for lateral movements, or movements to the side. Leg yielding is the most basic lateral movement. It usually takes place down the quarter line of the arena, a straight line halfway between the centerline and the outside track. The horse walks, trots, or canters down the quarter line while also moving toward or away from the rail. The horse's body should face straight forward while its legs cross diagonally in front of each other.

UPPER-LEVEL MOVEMENTS

Other dressage movements are found only at the highest levels. Horses must train for many years to be able to do them. Flying changes are when the horse switches from

leading with one leg to the other at the canter without going back to the trot. In counter canter, the horse canters on the left lead while circling the arena to the right, or vice versa. In canter pirouette, the horse pivots in a circle on one hind leg while still keeping the rhythm of the canter with its front end.

Passage is a dramatic, high-stepping trot that makes it look as if the horse is moving in slow motion. In *piaffe,* the horse slows its strides until it is trotting in place. Only the most athletic horses can perform piaffe.

THE DANCING HORSES OF AUSTRIA

The finest dressage in the world may be found at the Spanish Riding School in Vienna. The school uses Lipizzaner stallions. The most athletic stallions learn extremely difficult moves. The horse might leap into the air and kick out in capriole. Or it might rear up and hold that position like a statue in levade. This special training is called haute école, or high school. Today the Lipizzaners still perform for thousands of visitors to the Spanish Riding School each year.

Schianto, ridden by Sidsel Johansen, performs a canter pirouette on the right lead.

3

SCHOOL DAYS: TRAINING THE HORSE AND RIDER

The word "dressage" comes from the French word *dresser*, which means "to train." Most riders know the feeling of being on a horse that is not well trained. A lazy horse might buck when asked to go forward. An excitable horse might break into a faster gait without being asked. A horse might be trying to be good but gets distracted by the

Dressage teaches a horse to listen to its rider.

jumps in the corner of the arena. A solution for this can be dressage.

THE THEORY

In some horse sports such as trail riding, the horse moves along on a fairly loose rein. In dressage, the goal is to get the horse on the bit. This means the horse's mouth is in constant contact with the rider's hands. Many riders say that a special connection develops when the horse is ridden in this way. This is important, because horse and rider must have perfect communication in the ring.

The pyramid of training illustrates the six key elements of dressage. These are rhythm, relaxation, connection, impulsion, straightness, and collection. Rhythm means a horse's footfalls have energy and are timed consistently. Relaxation helps the horse bend. The horse does not tense with the rider's cues. Connection means the horse has accepted the bit. It stays in contact with the rider's hands. Impulsion is the controlled power in a horse's movement. It allows the horse to slow down its steps while keeping its energy, or to cover the ground in long, sweeping strides.

Straightness is a horse's ability to move evenly on both sides. Footfalls on the left happen with the same strength and length as footfalls on the right. Collection means getting the horse to step further under itself and shift

The pyramid of training helps the horse remain balanced and powerful as it performs movements such as extending its stride.

more of its weight to its hind legs. This requires strong muscles because a horse naturally carries more weight on its front end. A collected horse can turn on a dime or move easily from a halt to a canter and back again.

THE GROUNDWORK

Many dressage horses start their training by working on the lunge line, a long rope that clips to the horse's bridle. This can be done with or without a rider. The horse moves in a large circle around the trainer at the end of the lunge line. The horse usually wears its normal tack, or gear, while being lunged, or a special girth called a surcingle instead of a saddle.

Side reins that run from each ring of the horse's bit to the girth or surcingle mimic the feel of a rider's hands. Gradually the side reins are shortened until the horse's nose points more toward the ground. This helps the horse learn to carry itself on the bit without leaning on the reins. Lunging is also good practice for the rider. With a trainer controlling the horse from the ground, the rider can work without stirrups and reins to improve balance.

Gradually shortening the reins while lunging a horse teaches it to move with its nose tucked slightly.

HORSE AND RIDER

Any horse can compete in dressage, but some are bred for it. *Warmblood* is a general term for different types of large, athletic sport horses that are common in top-level dressage. The Dutch warmblood, Swedish warmblood, Hanoverian, Oldenburg, and Trakehner are popular warmblood breeds.

Other kinds of horses, such as Thoroughbreds, Friesians, and Arabians, can also excel in dressage. Quarter horses and Clydesdales can also be strong competitors at lower levels. Even ponies can compete. Two-time Olympian Lendon Gray had a 14.2-hand Connemara cross

While the medium-build warmbloods are popular for dressage, heavier horses including Friesians can also be very successful.

gelding, Seldom Seen. One hand is equal to 4 inches (10.2 cm). The pony won at the Grand Prix level and joined the USEF Hall of Fame in 2005.

YOUNG RIDER SPOTLIGHT

In 2016 Emma Claire Stephens became the youngest person to win a USDF silver medal. She was 11. When Emma started taking lessons, she tried several events before discovering dressage. Like many professional riders, Emma found sponsors to help fund the purchase of a horse, a 17-hand Dutch warmblood named De Nouvelle Vie. Emma's next goal is to compete with "Vivi" in the Dressage National Championships to earn her gold medal.

Dressage is sometimes seen as an elite and expensive sport. But there are opportunities for anyone who works hard to succeed. Many riders fund their shows with day jobs. Others take positions as working students for top dressage riders or teach lessons themselves. The qualities every dressage rider needs are patience, persistence, and the sensitivity to listen to the horse as well as give commands.

THE LEGENDS

Many great horses and riders have made their mark in dressage. Edward Gal and his stallion Totilas are a famous pair. In 2009, they became the first to score over a 90 percent in a dressage competition. The highest score possible is 100 percent. Gray is known for her success with Seldom Seen. She is also known for teaching all kinds of students, including children, older adults, and riders on horses without impressive pedigrees.

Some of the most famous dressage shows are the Rolex FEI World Cup, the FEI World Equestrian Games, and the CHIO Aachen horse show in Germany. As is true for many sports, competing in the Olympic Games is often seen as the highest achievement.

SHOW TIME: RIDING A TEST

Dressage shows are held at every level. Many riders start with schooling shows at local stables. These low-key competitions are a good way for riders to get experience without a lot of stress and expense. At USDF and FEI shows, the competition often lasts for several days. Riders may travel across the country or the world to compete.

Competitors should arrive at the show grounds with plenty of time to get themselves and their horses ready. After the horse is unloaded from the trailer and settled in, the first thing to do is find the show office or tent.

Local dressage shows are less stressful and less expensive, making them a good introduction to showing.

Each rider will get an entry number for their horse's bridle and their coat, along with their scheduled ride time. Some competitors might have to rush to get ready for an 8:00 a.m. test, while others will have to wait until late afternoon.

TACK AND TURNOUT

Horses should be carefully groomed for a show, with their whiskers clipped and white markings scrubbed clean. The horse's mane will be split into a dozen or more button-style braids. Tails are not braided for dressage.

Dressage tack is usually black or dark brown. The saddles have a deep seat and a long flap so the rider's leg can wrap around the horse's sides. The girth that keeps the saddle in place is short with elastic on both sides.

Horses can be ridden in a simple snaffle bridle or in a double bridle with two sets of reins at upper levels. The rider's whip and spurs must also be under a certain length. A ring steward checks each horse's tack to make sure these rules are followed for the horse's safety. The steward

Button braids expose a dressage horse's powerful, arched neck.

also looks over the horse for marks that would indicate that the horse has been trained harshly.

The rider's outfit for dressage is white or tan breeches, a white or light-colored show shirt, and a black or dark

DRESSAGE
GEAR

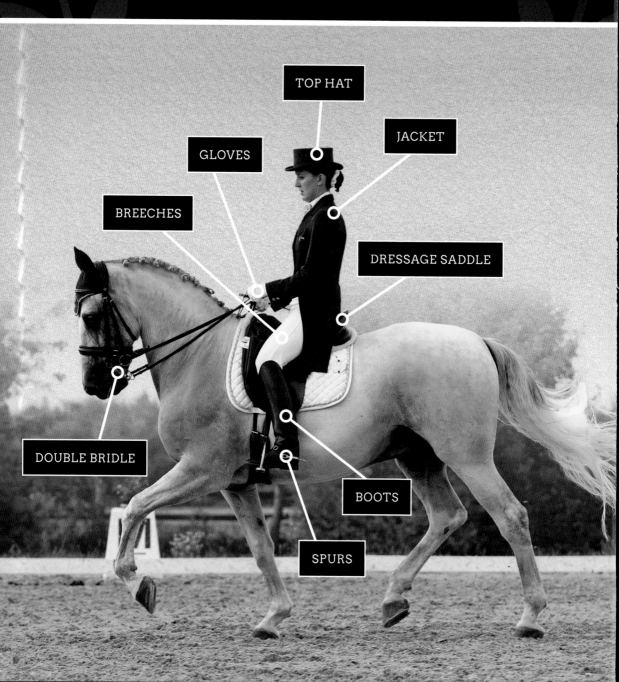

TOP HAT

JACKET

GLOVES

BREECHES

DRESSAGE SADDLE

DOUBLE BRIDLE

BOOTS

SPURS

show jacket. Gloves are white or match the jacket, and knee-high boots are black or match the jacket. At the highest levels, riders wear white gloves and a short coat with tails called a shadbelly. Many riders wear helmets, though advanced riders may wear a bowler or top hat.

TEST TIME

Every show has a warm-up area for horses to practice in before their tests. When it is a team's turn to compete, a bell rings to signal that the rider has either 45 or 60 seconds to enter the show arena, depending on the organization. Dressage rings come in two sizes: 65.6 feet by 196.9 feet (20 m by 60 m) and 65.6 feet by 131.2 feet (20 m by 40 m). The fence is made of low, white rails that a horse can easily step over. If all four of the horse's hooves leave the arena during a dressage test, the pair is eliminated.

Dressage arenas are marked with letters evenly spaced around the edge. Beginning at the entry gate and going right, the order for a lower level small arena is AFBMCHEK, with X in the center of the ring. There are 10 more letters

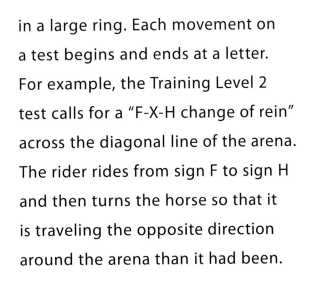

in a large ring. Each movement on a test begins and ends at a letter. For example, the Training Level 2 test calls for a "F-X-H change of rein" across the diagonal line of the arena. The rider rides from sign F to sign H and then turns the horse so that it is traveling the opposite direction around the arena than it had been.

The judge sits on a platform outside the arena facing the letter C. Some competitions may have up to five judges. Except in FEI shows, riders may have a reader who calls each movement out loud. Most riders memorize their tests.

The horse and rider begin their test by entering the arena down the centerline at A. It is easy for riders to

The letters around the ring are used to tell riders where to perform each movement.

get nervous under the judge's watchful eye, but the best strategy is to relax and focus on good communication with the horse. If the pair performs a wrong movement during the test, a bell rings, and the pair is eliminated.

Every dressage test ends with a halt and salute to the judge as a sign of respect. The rider puts both reins in the left hand and drops his or her right arm down straight while nodding to the judge.

The horse and rider can then leave the arena on a loose rein. The judge may offer a few words of advice or encouragement. After the ride, the horse should be walked to cool off, untacked, and offered a drink—and maybe a well-earned carrot.

Dressage tests also begin with a salute to the judge.

WHAT'S THE SCORE?

Each movement on a dressage test is scored individually. A score of 0 means the movement wasn't done at all. A 10 means it was done perfectly. The judge also awards

Charlotte Dujardin and Valegro perform a counter canter at the 2014 London International Horse Show.

5 collective marks for the horse's gaits, impulsion, and submission, and for the rider's position and correctness. Most riders are pleased with scores of 6s and 7s. A score of 8 is excellent, and 9s and 10s are very rare.

At the end of each test, the scores are added up to get a percentage of the total possible points. The horse and rider with the highest score win the competition. The judge also makes written comments on each test. This feedback helps the rider to know what to work on in training. The top six or 10 riders will get ribbons, with a trophy or other award for the first-place winner. Some competitions have cash prizes.

The record for the highest score on any USDF or FEI dressage test is a 94.3 percent. It was awarded to Charlotte Dujardin and her Dutch warmblood gelding Valegro for their musical freestyle at the 2014 London International Horse Show. As well as performing each movement almost perfectly, the pair truly looked as if they were dancing.

GLOSSARY

BIT
The mouthpiece of a horse's bridle, usually made of metal.

CANTER
A horse's three-beat gait that is faster than a trot but slower than a gallop.

CENTERLINE
The track in the exact middle of the arena, passing through the letters A-X-C.

DOUBLE BRIDLE
A bridle with two bits (a snaffle and a curb) and two sets of reins. A double bridle gives the rider extra control but requires skill to use correctly.

PEDIGREE
A written record of a horse's breeding over many generations.

RAIL
The outside track of the arena.

SNAFFLE
A kind of mild bit.

SPORT HORSE
A type of horse bred for dressage, show jumping, or three-day eventing.

TROT
A speed in between the walk and canter where the horse moves diagonal legs, such as the front right and back left, together.

WHIP
A long, flexible stick with a tassel on the end used to back up leg signals.

WORKING STUDENT
A rider who exchanges stable work for instruction from a well-known trainer and who may live on the trainer's farm during that time.

ONLINE RESOURCES

Booklinks
NONFICTION NETWORK
FREE! ONLINE NONFICTION RESOURCES

To learn more about dressage, visit **abdobooklinks.com**. These links are routinely monitored and updated to provide the most current information available.

MORE INFORMATION

BOOKS

Eschbach, Andrea. *Kids Riding with Confidence: Fun, Beginner Lessons to Build Trusting, Safe Partnerships with Horses*. North Pomfret, VT: Trafalgar Square, 2014.

Harris, Susan E. *The United States Pony Club Manual of Horsemanship: Basics for Beginners/D Level*. Hoboken, NJ: Wiley, 2012.

Sanderson, Whitney. *Intro to Eventing*. Minneapolis, MN: Abdo Publishing, 2018.

INDEX

ABOUT THE AUTHOR

Whitney Sanderson grew up riding horses as a member of a 4-H club and competing in local jumping and dressage shows. She has written several books in the Horse Diaries chapter book series. She is also the author of *Horse Rescue: Treasure*, which is based on her time volunteering at an equine rescue farm. She lives in Massachusetts.